# PRAYERS

# PRAYERS

BY

JENKIN LLOYD JONES

WIPF & STOCK · Eugene, Oregon

Wipf and Stock Publishers
199 W 8th Ave, Suite 3
Eugene, OR 97401

Prayers
By Jones, Jenkin Lloyd
ISBN 13: 978-1-5326-0157-6
Publication date 7/15/2016
Previously published by The Beacon Press, INC., 1927

## PREFACE

ARLY in the nineties with the intention of only catching them and preserving them for her personal benefit, Mrs. Annie Laurie Kelly, a member of All Souls Church, began to take down these prayers stenographically. Mr. Jones had no knowledge that this was being done, in fact did not hear of it until some years later. About 1912, he adopted the practice of preaching without manuscript and since that time the prayer as well as the sermon was taken down by his secretary, Miss May Johnson.

The Prayers contained in the following pages, edited and published at the urgent request of the author's friends, represent but a small number of those given by him during his ministry. But they are sufficient to show the range and depth of his spirit and the faith in which he worked and which stayed him through the years.

The Prayers, covering a period of some twenty-six years, are arranged preferably according to their thought content or the subject of the sermon which they preceded. That the reader may compare the same theme expressed at various intervals and under differing conditions, the title of the accompanying sermon and its date are given with each prayer.

The only introduction offered is indeed a
happy one. It is taken from his own sermon,
" Why Pray? " and with his characteristic insight
gives the most fitting approach to this collection.

EDITH LLOYD JONES

Abraham Lincoln Centre,
    Chicago.

# INTRODUCTION

# INTRODUCTION

OUTWARD things are easily discussed; those things which touch the surface of our life we may debate and at times laugh and joke about in public. Of our hopes and fears, our disappointments and discouragements we may hint in the sweet confidences of love. Still below these there is an unsurveyed region of reality, a world of yearnings and gropings, strengths and weaknesses that reveal their existence, if at all, not in words and phrases, but in glimmerings of joy or sorrow that mantle the face, in the tenderer tones, the firmer step, the kindlier smile, in unwonted flashes of eye-light. Prayer and Worship are words that point to these deeper strata of being.

"Prayer is the soul's sincere desire, uttered or unexpressed." It is the human reaching for the divine, not the divine stooping towards the human. I believe that the answer to every prayer is not according to our asking but according to our needs; not what we beg for but what we deserve. I believe in prayer because I must believe in human aspirations. I pray not because I ought to but because I must. Prayer is a part of the up-reaching and outreaching law of nature. Prayer is native to the soul first as tumultuous solicitation, eager petitioning, then divine aspiration, lastly splendid thanksgiving and glorious praise.

I believe in prayer because there is a prayer not born of fear, that is not craven obeisance; that is adoration, that is soaring on wings of gratitude, of admiration; that is communion with the pure. I pray because I cannot help it; it is an attitude of soul that is natural and at times inevitable. If we find a prayerless soul I think it must belong to one who has never known the agony sweat in any lonely Gethsemane, who has never entered the solitudes of a great purpose, who has never yearned for higher levels, never staggered under the crushing weight of unpopularity, that sought to wrench the mind from the simplicity of truth, — only such an one has never prayed.

Prayer is beautifully democratic. The peasant and the prince, the slave and the conqueror, aye, the murderer and the saint find common ground for their kneeling at the altar of worship, — and they are one and confess it. Whenever the cry goes out for forgiveness and sympathy the Father is everywhere present to greet the soul with a kiss. God is in every cry that goes Godward.

The most stalwart, tenderest, far reaching potency in human life is represented by the words ' father ' and ' mother '. So my spirit will climb on the trellis of speech to the Father of all and to the Mother heart, that gives us father and mother in the flesh. The pebble on the street touches Saturn. The ripple on the beach mates to the moon. The sea obeys the attraction and the

moon bends to the ocean and the ocean rises to
the moon. And so to every prayer there is an
answer before it is uttered. For —

> " In every, ' O my Father,' —
> Slumbers deep a, ' Here, my child '."

*From the Sermon on Prayer.*
Jenkin Lloyd Jones.

# CONTENTS

PREFACE .......................... v

INTRODUCTION — From the Sermon on
   Prayer. J. LL. J. ................ ix

SERIES ON EVOLUTION ............... 1

NATURE AND HUMAN NATURE ....... 7

SAINTS AND SAVIOURS .............. 15

OLD AND NEW TESTAMENT TEXTS ...... 27

MUSIC ............................ 47

MEN AND BOOKS .................. 53

CONFIRMATION CLASS .............. 69

FESTIVAL DAYS ................... 73

STUDIES IN MODERN MYSTICISM ....... 87

ANTI-WAR ........................ 95

FUNERALS ........................ 107

MISCELLANEOUS ................... 115

# SERIES ON EVOLUTION

# EVOLUTION

UNDER the shadows we know the sun shines; in the rain we think of cloudless sky. In our sorrow we lay hold of hope; out of our pain is born tenderness; out of our weakness we lay hold of strength, even thy strength, O thou infinite Father. Help us this morning, thou Spirit ever present, to read some sentences in thy book of revelation, written on the tablets of stone and the tablets of flesh. Help us to read the chapter in thy Gospel that tells of the coming of life and the development of the same. Help us to understand something of the architecture of our own bodies; the mystery, the power and the sacredness of the heart through which courses the blood; of the lungs where the air meets the wastages of life and through the mystery of nature, life is restored, strength renewed, mind cleared and life continued. Of all these things, Father, we would think this morning, and thinking, be led to feel the sanctities of the hour in which we live; the sacredness of the opportunities at which we have arrived; the inspirations that beckon us still onward and still upward to thee. Amen.

Physical—*From the Worm to the Biped.*
December 1st, 1912.

AY we strive ever for the success of love. Father, may we grope through ignorance toward knowledge, through our weakness toward strength, through our bitterness to love, through failure to trust. Help us to realize the solemnities in which we are cast. Help us to fear the pitfalls over, beneath, before and behind us. Grant that we may indeed feel thy creative impulse, the lure of thy creative love, the strength and power that thou dost pour into the lives of those who think thy thoughts after thee and grope through darkness into the light, through distrust and weakness into trust and strength evermore. Amen.

Psychical—*From Brawn to Brain.*
December 8th, 1912.

OUCH us this morning, O Father, with a consciousness of the brotherhood that binds us to the saints, the seers and the sages of all ages. Touch us with a sense of kinship with the frailest and weakest of our kind. May that touch, Father, quicken in our hearts the love of the brotherhood that now is. Lead us into the brotherhood of suffering that we may share with the burden bearers. Lead us into the brotherhood of the solitary and the lonely that we may give companionship and know the joys of comradeship. Lead us, O Father, into the brotherhood of gladness, that we may know the joy of life, the fullness of thy bounty, the

inspiration and the radiance about us. We pray
for the beckoning hand of the future, the call
to duty, the joy of service in the world. May our
prayers pass through the gateway of words into
the citadel of deeds, into the temple of life, that
with the living we may ever praise thee, who art
the living God, now and forever more. Amen.

Social—*From Tyranny to Democracy.*
January 5th, 1913.

INFINITE LOVE, help us to find thee.
Never failing love, help us to trust
thee. All sufficient power of love, help
us to find our strength in thee. O
Father, help us to climb through hate and
selfishness to the heights where love and disinterestedness bring peace in the midst of the
storm; rest in the strain of work; comfort in the
disappointments of life. Father, we are weak and
need some strong revealing of thyself this morning. May we find it in the upreaching of life
everywhere, and may the love that is resting in
the nest of the bird, in the home of the savage, in
the heart of the sage, be ours this morning, that
thy peace may come into our lives and thy
strength be found in our arms and thy truth find
utterance in our words. Amen.

Moral—*From Hate to Love.*
January 12th, 1913.

NFINITE NEARNESS, Infinite Mystery, thou art nearer to us than our own selves, and yet thou dost inhabit immensity. Thou art the thought of our thinking, and still thy ways are past finding out. Thou who art order and power and terror, and yet whose love encircles us, whose care protects us, whose providence guides us through darkness to the light, through weakness to strength, through doubt to trust, help thy children this morning to realize thy presence in the beauty about us and the yearnings within us. Help us, Father, to feel our kinship with the stars and to read the blush of shame upon our cheeks and the humility and guilt in our hearts. All are revelations leading us to the thing we ought to be. Father, our words fail, our sentences break, our songs falter, but in death as in life we are thine. In our ignorance as in our knowledge we would ever be consciously near thee, and still ever nearer to thee. Amen.

Religious—*From Fetishism to Theism.*
January 19th, 1913.

# NATURE AND HUMAN NATURE

## NATURE AND HUMAN NATURE

FILL our hearts with gladness this morning, Thou Spirit of Sunshine. Touch our souls with courage, O Thou Eternal Source of Power. Father, warm us with a loving yearning toward our kind, that still more we may find Thee under and through the clouds of adversity that overhang us; in the accumulated cruelties of men that so belie thee.

Father, help us to reach the light beyond the darkness, to rest in the sunshine that lies behind all shadows. Help us to feel thy presence in the flowers that bloom in unseen places, in the rivulets that trickle to enrich the ocean from unknown sources. Help us, Father, to feel thy love and thy law pleading to us in the cries of the orphan, the groans of the widow and the tortured agony of the dying.

Father, crown us this morning with the high commission; shame us into earnestness. Help us, Father, to forget the things that divide, that weaken, that exhaust for no good end, that we may better concentrate our powers on those things that abide. We would become worthy members of the forward-moving bodyguard of truth and love, pledged to fight with the weapons of gentleness, to conquer by patience and by love. Thus will thy kingdom come on earth as it is in Heaven. Amen.

Clouds—*An after vacation Sermon.*
September 27th, 1914.

FATHER, we are weak and need some deep revealing of hope and comfort from above. Father, when vision fails and courage weakens, help us to find faith and strength and comfort in the thought of the everlasting arms that are ever about us. In the confusion, the passion of the day, may we hear the still small voice that speaks of things eternal. Help us to realize that behind the darkest clouds thy sun doth shine, and after the fiercest tempest radiance and life and cheer will follow. Father, reveal to us our deeper needs, summon us this morning to our higher tasks, baptize us anew with courage to do and dare for those things that make for peace and power of the spirit, give us faith in things intangible. Help us to rest in the ideal. Give us courage to follow thee. Make us more willing workers so that we may hear more clearly thy summons to tasks high and tender, to service sweet and earnest. In the spirit of the brave ones who lived in times of turmoil and suffered that we might be freer, we would worship this morning that we may do better work and when need be, more patiently wait. Amen.

*Spiritual Forces*
October 11th, 1914.

HELP us, Father, once more to live in the vital rays of the sun. Gather us at this altar dedicated to service and to truth, that in our lives we may again testify to the goodness that overshadows us, the beauty that envelopes, the love that sustains us. Father, through us may the prayer for " peace on earth and good will to men " be embodied. So may thy law of progress be exemplified; so may the message of growth find new illustrations. Father, we consecrate ourselves anew to the service of truth and love and righteousness in the world. We would commit ourselves afresh to that unbroken fellowship that invites into this house of the Lord all struggling souls, all stumbling sinners, all aspiring loving, loyal hearts. Father, commission us afresh through the voice that speaks within the chambers of our own souls, to be the religion we profess, to practice the gospel we preach, to embody the laws we humbly confess. Make us more diligent workers in this garden of the Lord. Make us more earnest seekers in this college of the Most High. Baptize us with willing spirits; guide our feet, Father, in the paths of helpfulness. Touch our hands with tenderness and key our voices to kindly words. Amen.

*The Deforestation of Tower Hill.*
September 24th, 1916.

REVEAL thyself to us this morning, Father, in the radiance of the day, in the budding beauty of the season, but more — reveal thyself to us this morning in the radiant lives of thy chosen ones. Speak to us in the terms of motherhood today, help us to realize the burden of thy love revealed in father hearts. Help us to feel that we are in thy presence when we are in the presence of our brothers and sisters. We bless thee for the growing sense of comradeship, for the widening boundaries of the home, for the ever enlarging family. Father, may we know through thee the wealth of love that is ever flowing into the world through the gates of birth. Help us to realize that thou dost reconcile thyself to a wayward world in every new born child. We bless thee for babies. Help us to sing the cradle songs of trust and love to thee until thy love will over-flow the hearts of all men and hatred and rivalry shall cease. Amen.

Mothers—*A Peace Day Sermon.*
June 7th, 1914.

FOR the child we give thee thanks this morning, Father, for the continued renewal of life through the cradle we bless thee. For the spiritual revelation of life that thou hast given us in mother care and father devotion, we thank thee. May we be worthy of this inheritance. Hasten the day when the cradle song of the home shall become the home song of the world. Enable us to enlarge the boundaries of our firesides, open our hearts to love for all our kind, pluck out of our hearts the hatreds that so despoil the world, so desecrate the home, debauch life and profane infancy.

Father, may thy peace come through nobler living, through greater self-denial, through the companionship of love. Amen.

*The Heritage of Children.*
December 3rd, 1916.

IN the sanctities of the home we would find rest, Father. In the hallowed memories of the fireside we are strong. In the sacred leading-strings of Mother-love, in the sheltering care of Father-thought, we are ever led onward and upward to thee.

We thank thee for the holy influences of the home. We praise thee for the revelations of the fireside. Consecrate us, O Father, to the parental

obligations of life, that little children may heed
our words and may not be led astray when they
follow in our footsteps. Amen.

*Devout Homes.*
January 28th, 1917.

ELP us, Father, to interpret thy presence in rain as in sunshine. Help us
to bless thee for the showers that fer-
tilize, the winds that purify, the
doubts that strengthen. Round about us, Father,
is wrapped a mantle of ignorance. We cannot see,
we may not know, but we grope ever towards the
right, strive ever for the truth, stumble ever
towards the light. Strengthen us, cheer us, guide
us, guard us until we realize our common
brotherhood, our common burdens and our common duties. Amen.

*Thomas the Doubter.*
April 11th, 1915.

# SAINTS AND SAVIOURS

# SAINTS AND SAVIOURS

## Women Saints

SOURCE of light, Giver of love, Father of us all, help us to forget the things that separate and divide. Help us to rest in the thought of that fellowship that reaches through all the realms of life. Help us, thou Infinite Source of light, love and power, to give thee thanks for the mother spirit that giveth love and wisdom. We thank thee for the deep roots of the home, for the sweet consolations of the fireside, for the mighty inspirations of parenthood. We bless thee for the heritage of children. Through them dost thou reconcile a wayward world to thyself. We thank thee for the revelations of the cradle. Make us better children, Father, better guardians of the little ones. Under thee may we become the fostering providence that shall give to this world better children and men and women, that thy peace and power may come into our lives and through us into our community by the power of the hearthstone. Redeem the wayward spirits and reconcile the warlike nations one unto the other and all unto thee. Amen.

Rizpah—*Primal Motherhood*.
November 9th, 1913.

E, thy children of love, would fain advance the kingdom of love. Teach us, O Father, to see the better way and to walk therein. Give us this morning a glimpse of the power of the unarmed soul that stands for truth and justice, clad only in the armor of the spirit. Help us to lay aside and to leave behind the weapons of hate, the instruments of destruction, the armament of the lower and the baser life. Help us to live in the sunshine and spread the light that streams therefrom, that brother may recognize brother the world o'er and all men confess their kinship unto thee, the common Father of us all. Amen.

Boadicea—*The Woman Militant*.
November 16th, 1913.

HILDREN of the golden grain, children of the golden sunshine, we give thanks this morning to thee, the bountiful Father. For the rich garniture of garden and orchard, of field and of forest, we give thanks. For the holier fruitage of fireside, the nobler wealth of the family, the high fruitage of the heart, we give thee thanks this morning. For the still higher fruitage of the soul that bears the apples of heroic deeds, the wealth of self-denial, those achievements of conscience that make rich the glories of history, upon which thy struggling, stumbling, tender children may feed and renew their strength and refresh their souls, we give thee thanks.

For the season of Thanksgiving, Father, that takes note of autumnal wealth, of family joys, of national prosperity, we give thanks and we pray that this Thanksgiving season may so enrich our hearts that we may become conscious of the great board around which thou dost gather all thy children. Greek, barbarian, Jew and Scythian, — all are welcome, Father, around thy Thanksgiving board. For the larger fellowship, for the nobler purposes, for the higher aim and the broader vision we give thee thanks this morning. Amen.

Hypatia—*The Woman Sage*.
November 23rd, 1913.

THOU who art so far above and so far beyond, can we bridge that distance with words! May our phrases serve as a pathway over which the soul may travel to thee. Help us, thou Unspeakable, to speak the words of faith and hope and love. May they fall from our human lips in such a way that they may suggest the infinite fount of love out of which they spring, toward which they are turned. Thou who art infinitely near when words fail us and our phrases mock us, help us to open our own hearts and there recognize the revelations of that power that swings planets, tugs at our wills, rebukes our wilfulness, cheers our efforts, soothes our pains and disappointments. Father, we pray thee for the prayerful heart. We seek the trusting spirit, faith in things invisible. Amen.

Saint Monica—*The Woman Saint*.
November 30th, 1913.

ELP us, Father, to realize the besetting mystery of life. Help us to realize that we play upon the beach of an infinite ocean of truth and that thy wisest children can only pick up here and there a pebble. Touch us, O Father, with a sense of unseen realities. Bring us consciously into the presence of the verities that we cannot see, handle or touch, the verities that make our bodies lovable and our hands serviceable. Help us, O Father, to realize that beyond the near things that distract lie the permanent things that are most worth while, the things that longest endure. By such vision we will be crowned with the strength, time, resources material and spiritual to serve thee by serving thine. We pray, Father, for the peace that comes to those who dwell in thee. We pray for that divine leisure that enables the most hurried of souls to know the calm, the poise and the rest of those who feel that underneath them are the everlasting arms.

Help us, Father, to live in time for eternal causes; to give our days and hours to those things that abide. May thy kingdom come in our lives when they are devoted to thee and thy truth. Amen.

Joan of Arc—*The Woman Inspired.*
December 7th, 1913.

QUIET, Father, our wayward hearts, calm our feverish pulse; help us, O thou Infinite Presence, to stay our haste, to allay the ambitions that so burn, to put aside the prejudices and passions that so excite, that we may rest in the thought of things enduring, that we may concentrate our minds on things that last, that we may conserve our strength for things worth while.

Father, clear our vision that we may see that only those things are worth while which deal with permanent life, only those things are worth while which serve thy children, which lift them into communion with thee and harmony with one another.

Help us, Father, to catch with our senses the higher notes of the spirit, to detect with our earthly ears the Heavenly Song,—"Peace on earth and good-will among men." Guide us into the good wills of men, fill us with good-will toward men, help us by the light of thy noble ones to rededicate ourselves to the things that make for harmony, for progress, for purity, for helpfulness, for gentleness and love. Amen.

Susannah Wesley—*The Modern Woman.*
December 14th, 1913.

*Believing Heretics*

REVEAL to us, Father, the sanctities of life this morning. Touch us with a new sense of the sacredness of living. Help us to realize that thy touch is on every life and thy spirit moveth every soul. Help us, Father, to recognize our lowly origin that we may realize that thou hast raised thy prophets and thy saints out of the soil that gave us life. Help us to realize that we are brothers and sisters to those bright ones who made life noble and rich by sacrifice, who glorified the day in which they lived by giving of their lives to truth, to beauty, to justice. Amen.

*Pelagius.*
January 11th, 1914.

THOU Comforter of bruised hearts, Thou Companion to the lonely, Consolation to the disappointed, Strength to the humble, — we come with our broken plans and bruised hearts, we come with our disappointments and defeats to that altar whereon blooms the Eternal Presence which is everywhere, to that Presence which reveals the eternal, which is always. We come, Father, seeking courage to hear the things we deem right. We come, Father, seeking the gentle heart, the tender spirit, the kind word and the helping hand that indicate the " peace that passeth understanding," the peace that alone comes to those who

rest in thee, who feel that beneath them are the
" everlasting arms " and that above them is forever and forever the over-arching love. Amen.

Roger Williams. 17th Century.
January 25th, 1914.

## Christian Pathfinders to Peace

N the solemnity of this new day, the
majesty of the sunlight and the mystery of our human hearts, we fain
would realize thy presence, Father of
us all. Help us to realize that we are standing in
the " foremost files of time," a boundless past
behind us and an endless future before us. Touch
us with a sense of the value of effort, the sanctity
of life, the divinity of toil. Guide us out of the
paths of violence into the ways of peace; lead us
out of hatred into love. Amen.

Saint Benedict—*The Road of Labor.*
March 19th, 1916.

WE thank thee, Father, for the many paths that lead to thee. We would give special thanks for the illumined path-finders who, with prophetic vision, have led the way to the citadels of love and peace, aye, for those who have illumined the dark places of life, those whose words cheer us in hours of fatigue and discouragement, whose deeds encourage us in moments of doubt and distrust. May we show our gratitude to thee, Father, as we travel along the highways that lead to peace and brotherhood, by becoming each in his own way, pathfinders, pathmakers to thee. Amen.

Michael Angelo—*The Road of Beauty*.
April 2nd, 1916.

IN our weakness we would rest in thy strength, in our hatreds we would find thy love, in our ignorance we would seek thy wisdom, in our loneliness we would find companionship with thee, Infinite Nearness, Ever Present Order, Dominating Law and Conquering Love. Thou who hast worked through all the ages, who holdest sway through all changes and dost abide ever in our hearts, dost answer our crying and meet our wants before we realize them, we pray thee to strengthen and comfort us, and guide us in the paths of peace and the ways of love forevermore. Amen.

Thomas a Kempis.
April 9th, 1916.

IN the solemnity of this place, the beauty of this day with the high causes of this generation in mind, we would worship this morning. Help us, O Thou Eternal Wisdom, to trust the wisdom that is given us out of the pages of history, out of the testimony of thy chosen ones, and declared in the chambers of our own souls. Infinite source of love that broods over the bird's nest and guides the nest builder, teach us also to love. O Thou Infinite Energy that swings the planets and keeps them in their courses and brings the flowers in their season, give us of thine own strength, renew our courage and direct our energies along the paths that lead to the triumph of the spirit, and the dominion of mind, the reign of law, forevermore. Amen.

Sir Thomas More—*The Road of Reason.*
April 16th, 1916.

# OLD AND NEW TESTAMENT TEXTS

# OLD AND NEW TESTAMENT TEXTS

## Beginnings

ALM our feverish hearts, this morning, Father, — check our mad haste and wild impatience. Reveal to us the slow and sure workings of thy will; restore our faith in human kind; lift us out of our prejudices; teach us to love those from whom we differ; sanctify this great test that has been brought to thy people in this land of promise. Abate our hatreds, reduce our antagonisms, strip us of our dogmatisms, that we may realize that thy struggling children of every name and age and party are thy children and our brothers and sisters, dwelling in the one homeland, members of the one family circle. Sweeten our lives today and tomorrow and the great days after that. Amen.

Genesis—*Beginnings. The Pre-Human World.*
November 5th, 1916.

NTO the beauty of a new day we come, Father; into the glory of the hour that now is, we enter; may we also enter consciously into the sublime responsibilities of life. May we heed the beckoning hand that would lure us to our opportunities to serve thee and thine. Lift us, O God, out of the narrow and selfish path into the broad road of truth and justice. Help us to feel the common life that surges about us and through us. Help us to realize the aeons back of us, lifting us age by age into the sunlight, guiding us generation after generation into the paths of peace and the ways of righteousness. Give us courage, Father, to face the future. Give us energy to do our duty; clarify our minds, free us from prejudices and bigotry; purify our hearts, cure them of their hatred and bitterness. Make us loving and loyal, that we may go forth from this place better children of thine, truer workers in thy vineyard. Amen.

*The Advent of Man.*
November 12th, 1916.

MAY the holy endeavors of the past come to us this morning with lessons of courage and hope. May the radiance of this hour give us courage to look forward. We bless thee, Father, for the tides of love that come down to us through unnumbered centuries, groping through the darkness of ignorance, struggling over the bitternesses and hates of life, revealing to us age after age the better way, teaching us generation through generation that the paths of love are the paths of power; that the ways of peace are the ways of holiness. Make us righteous within, purge our hearts of hatred, clear our minds of ignorance that we may be one with thy holy ones of all ages, one with thee, one with all mankind now and forever. Amen.

*The Advent of Woman.*
November 19th, 1916.

## The First Table of the Law Brought Down to Date

AY the unseen realities impress us this morning; may the hidden powers quicken us, may the Holy Presence within reveal itself to us. Father, help us to rise above the distractions of the hour, to look beyond the things that glitter and that too often attract the attention of our brief days here on earth. Help us to ally ourselves with things eternal, to feel thine infinite Presence. O Father, help us to realize that now and here is thy Presence. May thy peace come into our lives that through us thy message of peace may be borne to the feverish and distracted world. Still the passions of men; check the impetuous ambitions of the hour; touch us all with a sense of the sacredness of life and the holiness of death. Amen.

*Devout Thinking.*
*"Thou Shalt Have No Other Gods Before Me."*
January 7th, 1917.

THOU who occupiest immensity, who fillest eternity, yet art present in the contrite heart and moving in the humble spirit, thy majesty is revealed to us day by day, the glory of the heavens breaks upon us, the radiance of thy sun and the revelation of the snowflakes alike speak to us of the littleness of life and the majesty of spirit, the brevity of our years and the eternity of our hopes. Quicken us, strengthen us, sweeten us, chasten us, Thou Spirit of all Good, Source of all Life. Amen.

*Devout Speaking.*
January 14th, 1917.

IN the solemn shadows of this hour we turn to the light that never fails and find the glory that pierces every cloud and shines behind that which makes the shadows. Remembered today be our fellows in suffering and bonds, remembered this day be the lonely and desolate. We would share with them the joys of life, rejoice with them in the sympathies of love, the inspirations of duty. May we be the better for having been here. Restore our souls as well as our bodies, refresh our minds as well as our limbs. Speak to us in the sublimities of history, the traditions of the ages, the radiant lives of holy saints. Amen.

*Devout Helps.*
*Holy Days and Places.*
January 21st, 1917.

## The XXIII Psalm

ELP us, Father, in our search for things lasting, in our quest for the power that fails not, in our pursuit of deathless things. Forbid our empty phrasing, but lead us into the highest sanctity of the silences where ever broods the ineffable. Amen.

*Theism Brought Down to Date.*
*Where is the Shepherd?*
May 7th, 1916.

ELP us to find thee, Father, in the gracious and benignant order of nature, the bountiful sunshine, the creative rain, the unbroken and unfailing message of the seasons. And none the less, help us to find thee in the ungraciousness of providence, as interpreted by our halting minds and our inadequate experiences. Help us to find thee in the woes as well as in the joys of life, in the agonies as well as in the ecstasies of soul. Father, reveal thyself to us in the lashings of the spirit, the tortures of conscience, the hunger of the human heart, so that through our very waywardness we may be brought to thee. Amen.

*The Hound of Heaven.*
*God In Hell.*
May 21st, 1916.

THOU who inhabiteth Eternity, may we hear thy voice speaking in our own souls, see thy purposes revealed in the mighty swing of the planets, and thy word established in the long events of history. Speak to us this morning, Father, in the near duties; help us to lift ourselves into the eternal presence of things that abide, that we may be healed of the wounds that weaken us, that we may find thee again, working in the dark ways of providence, guiding, checking, rebuking, punishing. Still thy law abides, thy words survive through the ages, and thy will alone endures. Amen.

*A Psalm of the Inner Life.*
*The Shepherd—God.*
October 1st, 1916.

PEN our hearts this morning, Father, that we may comprehend the deeper meaning of life; that we may get some intimation of the distinctions between things transient and things permanent. We would yield our minds and our hearts to thee that the tuition of the ages may find us and the discipline of life may grow more clear. Help us to realize, O Father, that thy ways are in the dark, that thy thoughts are not our thoughts, but that we are sheltered in thy breast, guided by ways we know not of toward the light and into the life of the spirit, which is the life of thought, the life of love, the life of duty.

We thank thee for the disciplines of life; the hard frosts of winter as well as the balmy breezes of summer which help clothe the earth with beauty. And so, through the chills of pain and disappointment, as well as the smile of appreciation and the encouragement of companionship, lead us ever nearer and nearer to thee, the Infinite Justice, the All-embracing Love, the Unlimited Permanence. Amen.

Discipline—*The Rod and the Staff*.
October 15th, 1916.

AY the beauty and majesty of life break in upon us this morning. May our words lead into the silences too profound for human speech. May our songs melt into a harmony not to be reproduced by human voices. May our hungerings outreach our arguments and our lives belie our doubts. May thy peace, Father, the peace that passeth understanding, the peace that is now and evermore, be ours this day. Amen.

Immortality—*The House of the Lord*.
October 29th, 1916.

## The Gospel in Parables

WE thank thee, Father, for the sowing time. We would hear, O Father, the message of these growing days. Open our eyes that we may behold thy creating hand touching the landscape into green, breaking into buds and blossoms on every bough. Help us to feel the springtime in our hearts and the call of the waiting fields in our souls. Make us co-workers with thee. May we lend to thy providence the hand necessary to plant and to sow. Help us to carry on the work of creation under thee. Make this world more fertile, more beautiful, more peaceful, more divine day by day, world without end. Amen.

*The Sower.*
April 20th, 1913.

WE see, Father, the better way. We wander towards the light and hunger for the right. Strengthen us in our pursuit, encourage us in our quest, enable us to feel that the ways of helpfulness are the ways of peace; that the hand that leads to service leads to thee, that the road to Heaven is the road to a neighbor's need and a brother's wants. We offer our reluctant spirits to thee this morning; make them more willing. We offer our clouded minds this morning; clear them, Father. We offer to thee our faltering wills; strengthen them that now and evermore we may be near and nearer to thee by being dear and still dearer to thee. Amen.

*The Good Samaritan.*
May 4th, 1913.

ATHER, help us to cast abroad the seed; help us to dig the well; help us to speak the word, that in thine own good time and in thine own good way will bear fruit, slake the thirst of countless children of thine; strengthen the heart of some brother or sister in need of refreshment.

Father, open our eyes to the opportunities around us, open our hearts to the call ever near. Open our hands and our purposes that the accumulations of life may be sped on their way doing good, helping the weak, healing the sick, soothing the discouraged and ever bringing thy wandering children home to thee. Quicken our consciences that we may serve thee by serving thine; that we may confess our faith in thee by testifying to thy truth more and more abundantly, forevermore. Amen.

*Dives and Lazarus.*
June 1st, 1913.

REVEAL to us this morning, Father, thy Fatherhood. Help us to catch glimpses of the tenderness into which thou hast placed us. Give us an increasing sense of the comradeship with which thou hast invested us. We pray for the family of man, for the brotherhood of nations. We pray for our struggling, stumbling kind, with whom and for whom we would evermore work. Help us to forgive as thou dost ever forgive. Help us to forget the things that hurt, the bitterness and the anger, that we may live in the sunshine of thy providence and in that light lead the march of history, which shows more and more clearly day by day, the message of love and not of hate, of gentleness and not of force, of mildness and not of bitterness. Make us more gentle that we may be better children of thy sunshine. Amen.

*"Our Debts."*
October 19th, 1913.

*Jesus*

ESETTING mystery, all enveloping power, source of light and love, in whom we live and move and have our being, we would be touched this morning with new faith in the triumphing power of truth and justice. We would be consoled this morning with a reinforcement of our confidence that justice and love will triumph in time and eternity. Touch us with a sense of the brotherhood that over-reaches battle lines, that overlays the contentions of men. May our ears be open this morning to hear the sweet music of hope and trust and love. Recommit us, Father, to the thought of brotherhood, world inclusive, without end. Amen.

*The Founder of Christianity and the
Master of Men, as He Appeared
to His Contemporaries.
The Carpenter's Son.*
May 9th, 1915.

UR Father, through the dissonance of the day may we hear the low, sweet music of eternity. Above the clouds of battle-smoke may we catch the rays of the unfailing sun. Beneath the bitterness of war may we discover the sweet harmonies of peace. The battle cry of the soldier is of the hour; the prayer of the mother is of the ages. Free us from the blindness, bitterness, foolishness that still believes violence more potent for justice than gentleness. Shame us out of the cowardice that leads us to tremble in the presence of the cannon's open mouth. Rather may we tremble in the presence of outraged homes and violated women.

Free us, Father, from the tyranny of creeds, of race and of language when these would limit our vision, harden our hearts and make bitter our spirits against our brothers and sisters who with equal sincerity seek protection under other flags and find inspiration in other battle-cries than ours. O God, muster us into the larger brotherhood, enable us to hold our ground on the battle lines where love and not hate is the inspiration.

Give us as a nation power to endure and if need be to die rather than wield the sword of violence in the name of the God of Love. Make us peaceable, make us citizens of the world, that we may help bring in the kingdom of love that knows no boundary lines save those of truth and justice. May our patriotism be of heaven and our " chosen land " be the land of peace where the kingdom of the righteous is established and the rule of the loving is supreme. Amen.

*As He Appears in History.*
*The Christ of the Creeds.*

May 23rd, 1915.

NTO the beauty of another day, the wealth of another week, we come, Father. Out of the fatigue, the distractions, the perplexities and the complications of life we come into the calm of worship, into the peace of this hour dedicated to thought. Lift us, Father, above the things that pass, to the heights where are the things that remain, where thy truth and love and law abide for which thy children ever seek. Help us, Father, to find the things that endure. Above all we would be guided by the deathless spirit of him who " went about doing good," his kindly heart, his independent will, his seeking mind and his open hand.

These, Father, may we seek, and finding them, find thee and the strength and renewal that mark the triumphs of thy chosen ones. Amen.

*As He Survives in the Hearts of Men.*

June 6th, 1915.

*Men of the New Testament*

N the joy of a new year, in the conscious benedictions of new opportunities, in the humiliations of things undone that we might have done, in humble penitence for the things neglected, we come, Father, hoping to catch new courage, to find new vision, and to lay hold of life anew as if it were fresh from thy hand, breaking upon us in strangeness, in glory, in infinite power. Amen.

*John the Beloved.*
January 3rd, 1915.

OR the light after darkness we give thee thanks. For the light out of darkness we give thee thanks. For the joys that come to the souls of those who serve thy suffering ones we give thee thanks. Lead us, O Father, into the service of truth. Recommit our faiths to things intangible, make us messengers of love, missionaries of brotherhood. Amen.

*Barnabas the Missionary.*
January 17th, 1915.

ATHER, we thank thee for the revelation of thyself in the life that now is. We thank thee for the witnesses to truth and life about us. We thank thee for that divine attraction that draws us toward things excellent that warm our hearts; toward love for things true and noble.

We thank thee, Father, that amid the stumblings and blunderings of man, the tide of life ever bears souls onward and upward. We thank thee that thou hast taught us that men do rise on the stepping stones of their dead selves toward thee. We thank thee for the glimpse that comes now and then of the inspiring truth that error is transient, truth permanent; evil ever floats on the surface but righteousness is ever deposited below.

Help us this morning to enter into the communion that knows no limits, the fellowship that defies boundaries, aye, even the lowest boundary we call Hell. In the life eternal we rejoice now and evermore. Amen.

*Titus the Missionary.*
February 7th, 1915.

ELP us this morning, O Father, into that loyalty that " Stands the cross beside." Give us the open vision to see things most worth while. Give us the courage to stand by causes unpopular. Give us vision that we may be willing to put ourselves in the minority. Give us to believe that thy triumphs come in the lives of men when they dare endure. Give us new faith in the power of love. Make us more valiant defenders of the unarmed Christ, that peace may come into our lives, into our homes, into our distracted city and throughout the war ridden world. Amen.

*Women of the New Testament,*
*of the Gospels.*

April 18th, 1915.

# MUSIC

## MUSIC

NFINITE source of harmony and beauty, breathe thy spirit upon us this morning. Father, lead us away from discord and strife, draw us to that which is above hatred, narrowness and selfishness into the realm of things eternal, into the presence of loyalties supernal, into that kingdom of love that abides, that realm of thought in which are found calm and rest.

We pray, Father, that we may lend ourselves to the ministrations of harmony, the interpretations of melody, by those whose speech breaks into song and whose lives bloom into hymns. We thank thee for the beauty-makers, we thank thee for the interpreters of the unseen. When sight fails thou dost visit the inner chambers of our ears; we hear the melody we cannot express, the harmonies we cannot live. We thank thee, Father, for the life that is not yet ours. We thank thee for the peace we have not yet attained, for in these we feel the lure of thy spirit. Thou art the God and Father of us all. Amen.

*The Organ.*
*Its Story and Message.*
April 15th, 1917.

ATHER, may thy blessing be consciously felt this morning. Help us to rise above the things of time and dwell for a moment where abideth the Eternal. Help us to rise to those heights from which the soul catches glimpses of things infinite. May we feel this morning the inspiration of the ages, be touched with the melodies that are from on high as interpreted through thy prophets of harmony. We bless thee for the power of song, we glorify thee for the rest that comes from music. Attune our hearts to the melodies of heaven this morning that we may be grateful for the masters of tone; thy interpreters in the tunes of the ages, the anthems of the generations, the psalms that die not. Amen.

*Johann Sebastian Bach.*
April 22nd, 1917.

ELP us to hear the heavenly music this morning, Father; to touch the tones of that conquering flute that sounds the notes of love. Help us to rise above hate, bitterness and war's degradations. Help us, Father, to climb the mount of love. From the Olivets of the heart we may hear the celestial music that through the ages has charmed the savage breast, soothed the discouraged spirit, strengthened the weak, comforted the forlorn and given conquering power to the meek. O God of Love, the Father of all men, the keeper of the temple of peace, in the spirit of the ages, in the conscious presence of the prophets of love, help us to worship thee. Amen.

*Wolfgang Amadeus Mozart.*
April 29th, 1917.

E ask not that for us the clouds be swept away, nor that for us the bitter blasts be tempered, but we do ask, O Father, that we may know that thy sun shines behind the darkest clouds and that after winter blasts come spring buds and summer fruits. We ask that we may bear thy burdens of discipline and pain that come in the benignant order of that nature which we poorly understand and rudely condemn. We ask that through sorrow, disappointment, unsatisfied hunger and ungratified desires we may catch the heavenly notes that come from the beyond and the above, the hearing of which will give to us the power to sing the Hymn of Joy. Help us to live as we would die in the thought of thy deathless love. Give us strength to bear our burdens to the grave and the beyond as thy cheerful, trustful children. Amen.

*Ludwig von Beethoven.*
May 6th, 1917.

# MEN AND BOOKS

# MEN AND BOOKS

## *The Three Deadly D's of Ruskin*

THOU INFINITE JUSTICE, we humble ourselves before thee, this morning. We confess our selfishness, regret our weakness and pray for a renewal of that faith that will enable us still to seek, still to strive with thy help " to rise on stepping stones of our dead selves " to better things. We humble ourselves before thee this morning, O Thou Infinite Beauty, and confess that we have marred the harmony, wrought discord where melody ought to be; harbored things unsightly that ought to be touched with infinite beauty. Give us courage to resist the temptations that are near, to lay aside the fetters of convention when they hold us to that which retards thy kingdom of brotherhood and sisterhood. Hasten the day, O Father, that will through our heroism, bring in the time of more justice, when none shall go naked in the presence of those who are over-clothed; none shall go hungry in the presence of those who are over-fed; none shall go idle in the presence of those who are over-worked. Make this prayer a sincere one. Our sincerity can be proven alone by our effort, and our prayer will be justified only by our deeds. Give us that dependency upon thee that will make us independent of the wayward ways of man. Amen.

*Dress.*
January 26th, 1913.

ELP us, Father, to feel the burden of the world this morning. Help us to realize our share therein. We bow before thee and in humility confess our waywardness. How often, Father, do we do the thing we know ought not to be done. How often have we chosen the path of dalliance rather than the path of self control. How often have we the favored, stumbled and wandered, to the confusion of the weaker ones who follow where we ought not to have led. Help us to realize that under thee we are appointed to lead in the way of sobriety, of self control. Help us to stand more loyally by the convictions that are ours; to dare live the life we espouse and practice the creed we confess. Tutor us by shame and humiliation out of the weaknesses that beset us. Hasten the day when the dark clouds of despair, the weak expenditure of life and money on things that are not worth while, will cease, that thy kingdom of sobriety may come, thy kingdom of self control, which is ever a Kingdom of Justice. Amen.

*Diet.*
February 2nd, 1913.

ATHER, have mercy upon thy wandering and wayward children. Guide us in our stumbling. We grope in the darkness, our vision is weak, our minds are confused, our consciences oftentimes fail to discern thy will in the complexity of our own interests. Help us to rise on the heights of prophecy until we may see the future beckoning us into the land of peace and harmony. O Father, use our voices that they may calm the turbulent turmoil of earthly passions. Help us to bring in that day promised by thy chosen ones in all times and all lands, when the " war drums shall beat no longer, when the battle flags shall be furled in the parliament of men and the federation of the world." Give us to see that thy truth alone is omnipotent, and thy will needs not the violent expression of human hate and rivalry. Thou dost but ask of thy children loyal living, patient waiting upon the dictates of what is true and righteous altogether. Help us to regard the claims of justice and knowledge, of sobriety. Give us a sense of that love that is loyal and that trust that is obedient to thy voice as revealed in the slowly unfolding pages of civilization, as revealed in the gory fields of battle, where the wastages of life cry up to heaven for reconciliation. Help us to serve thee and thee only, knowing that thou art the God of all thy children. Help us to bring about the time when all nations will recognize their kinship and all nations will bow before thee, Infinite Love and Eternal Justice. Amen.

*Debt.*

February 9th, 1913.

*Miscellaneous*

ATHER, make a " song of joy " our ex-
perience today. Open our eyes to the
glory of the world in which we live,
unstop our ears that we may hear the
harmonies, the promise, the prophecy all round
us. Touch our hearts with tenderness, that we
may feel thy love breaking through and disin-
tegrating the rocks of hate. Touch our hearts
again, Father, with a sense of our kinship to the
brotherhood that links us to the farthest and the
weakest, the meanest and the poorest. Father,
help us to realize that in these obscure ways thou
dost work thy purpose. Make us better brothers,
braver defenders of the right, more valiant rep-
resentatives of love, heroic witnesses to the ties
that bind and the calls to duty that ever lure us
onward, upward, nearer and ever nearer to thee.
Amen.

> *The Auto-Biography of a Super-Tramp.*
> William H. Davies.
>> October 14th, 1917.

FATHER, in the freedom of truth we come this morning, hoping that by the guidance of that spirit we may come into thy kingdom of love. We pray for love; deep, abiding, enduring love, not only for those near and dear to us in the mergence of time and the limitations of space, but we would know something of that divine love that reaches out beyond kin and country. We would realize something of that fatherly love that embraces not only the radiant children of light but the floundering sons of darkness. We would seek that love that penetrates the deepest hell, that broods over the most wayward children of man.

Father, make this place a temple dedicated anew to universal brotherhood. Give us patience in hours of darkness; give us courage in the face of discouragement. Help us to keep burning the light that is set upon a hill, that perchance it may show the way to some wandering child of thine to the Holy City which we would help build. Amen.

*Above the Battle.*
Romain Rolland.
October 21st, 1917.

NVARIABLE, irresistible, ever present, ever working Father of Souls, chasten our lives this morning with humility. Touch our hearts with a sympathy born of the sense that thou art Father of us all. Quicken our minds with the thought of thine own infinity, that we children of an hour, passing children of time and of earth, may find ourselves children of eternity, partakers of the everlasting love, the life that is all love. We would feel our kinship this morning with the worm that crawleth and the saints that beckon us. Help us to rise from the sweet communions of the kinships of the fireside and of the country into holy kinship with angels.

Touch us with the solemnities of life, the profundities of being, the realities beneath the shifting sands. We pray for a realizing sense of the abiding brotherhood, that which not only obliterates the distinctions between continent and continent and race and race, but between time and eternity. Yea, weakness and sickness and death itself cannot keep us out of this fellowship that belongs to thy children, O thou infinite Father of us all. Amen.

*Raymond.* Sir Oliver Lodge.
October 28th, 1917.

ELP us, Father, to feel the radiance that comes to us through the enkindling lives, the kindly faces and the warm hearts of thy chosen ones. Help us to realize that thy sun shines on the darkest days, that beauty abides at the heart of things when times are most turbulent and when nature seems ill at ease. Help us to feel things permanent, to rejoice in things that endure. We would abide in the tabernacle of the Most High where dwelleth forever things that are true and of good report, things that are just and full of mercy. Amen.

*Robert Collyer. A Preacher in the Sunshine.*
December 2nd, 1917.

HE tides of history bear us aloft this morning; the current of human destiny carries us in its bosom. The lives of the nameless saints are in our lives. The triumphs of the forgotten spell our privileges and bring to us the plenty which we graciously accept. Father, help us to feel the trials of the past, the struggles of our fore-elders, aye, the sufferings and the sacrifices of our fathers and our mothers. Teach us to revere the brave uncles and the splendid aunts, who toiled that the wilderness might bloom as a rose, who died that the wild grasses of the prairie might give way to the greater beauty of barn, farm and home yards. Touch, O God, our hearts with a sense of humili-

ation this morning, that we may realize how selfish and ungrateful and unthoughtful we are.
Teach us to feel that we are the partakers of their
bounty, the inheritors of their tears. Amen.

*Heroes of the Farm.*
A Study of Hamlin Garland's
*A Son of the Middle Border*
December 16th, 1917.

ATHER, into thy rest we would come
this morning; towards thy peace we
would travel. Father, heal the broken
hearts of the hour, sustain the fainting
souls, fortify the inquiring minds. May outward
serenity calm the turbulent hearts within. May
we rest in the thought of the Infinite. May we
stay our hearts in the presence of the ever unfolding life of the universe.

We remember the distracted nations, the broken homes, the young lives called from the shelter
of home and the guidance of society to face the
dangers and temptations of war. Father, be with
them, renew their faith in thee, touch them still
with divine brotherhood that encircles the world.
Use our tongues, our hands and our feet on
missions of love, ameliorate the hates of the world,
enkindle the love that illuminated the prophets,
that sustained the martyrs, that has enabled in-
vestigators to brave torrid heats and arctic cold,
strengthened discoverers to spend vigilant nights
watching the stars and seeking the secret of the

atom. Lift us this morning into the company of
the glorious life-savers and life-givers. Vouchsafe
to us a vision of things that ought to be, lest our
faith grow dim and our hearts grow cold. Help
us to find these in the near agonies of life, in the
inner storms of the spirit, in the struggling, aspiring, praying soul itself. We ask not for escape
from the turmoil and the trials of the world but
we ask that we may be enabled to carry our burdens in such a way as will approve itself to the
God within, to the God of history, the God of the
prophets and of prophecy that thy kingdom may
come here on earth, in our homes, in our nation, in
thy world. Amen.

*Borderlands.*
*Studies of the Besetting Mysteries*
*God, the Invisible King.*
H. G. Wells.

October 7th, 1917.

## Mark Twain's Gospel of Life

N the joys of life we worship, in the
conscious radiance of the power of
right and the power of truth we would
worship this morning. May the lives
of the cheerful ones shame our gloom, dispel
our discouragement. Though the things of the
hour be discouraging, the things of the centuries
inspire; though the hatred of man o'ercloud us,
Father, reveal to our inner sight the love of men.
Help us to worship in tune with mother hearts,
childish loves, fatherly cares. Help us on this day

of peace, in this hour of worship, in this place dedicated to brotherhood, to reaffirm our loyalty to thee, the God of Love. Forgive us for our hatreds, overrule our passions, consecrate our thoughts. Help us to dedicate ourselves anew to reason and to the faith that the laws of right are in league with the laws of reason and that the God of Life is in league with the Father of Love. Amen.

*Mark Twain, the Humorist.*
April 7th, 1918.

FATHER, help us to set our will to thine that we may find our peace in thee. Beset by the tumultuous waves of passion and temptation, of anger and fear, of wild hatred and high intent, help us to find the calm within the storm, the strength and peace at the heart of the tumult. We need not travel far to find thee. We need not search the pages of sacred scripture to know thy will which is written in our own hearts, revealed in the tumultuous experiences of the ages, voicing itself in the broken accents, in the agonies of the community, in that conscience that will not be silenced, in that life of the common company of men and women that ever overarches our own lives, pre-empts our own energies and enlists our wills if not by persuasion then by holy coercion.

We remember this morning the pain at the heart of society, the unrest that stretches through the community. We remember the peace that passeth all understanding that comes ever and anon to give thy beloved sleep. In this remembrance we worship this morning. Amen.

*Mark Twain in Business.*
April 14th, 1918.

FATHER, teach us to worship thee in spirit and in truth this morning. In the spirit of love and the courage of truth, the truth that maketh free, the truth that releases us from the bondage of outward standards, free from human limitations or oppositions, free in the companionship of the universal spirit, free in the forefront of human progress. Pluck out of our hearts this morning all hatred, shame us out of our narrowness, baptize us, O Father, anew with a fresh spirit of brotherhood, touch our hearts with a sense of gratitude for the brave prophets of the past, the fearless leaders of men, that we too may have courage to walk alone if need be with thee, to stand alone, if need be, with thy chosen prophets. So use us, this morning, Father, that we may live tomorrow, members of the great brotherhood of man, lovers of thy created beings, worshippers in thy ineffable presence. Amen.

*Mark Twain, the Prophet.*
April 21st, 1918.

ELP us, unseen, everpresent Reality, to see through the shame and passing lights of the day the lasting realities of Eternity. Help us in the consciousness of things fleeting, the moving panorama of earthly life, to know that there are those verities rooted in the eternal that abide forever. Give us a sense of kinship with the immortals, help us to realize our relationship with the forces that abide and the love that endures through all times, through all realms. Help us to a humble sense of our ignorance, reveal to us our limitations, help us, O Father, where the light fails, still to praise thee in weakness and when there seems no more to do within the reach of our poor human will, still may we realize that " they also serve who only stand and wait." Give us patience when all else fails, when vision ceases. Amen.

*Mark Twain, the Prophet of the Home.*
May 5th, 1918.

E pray for that freedom that truth alone gives, freedom from the blindness of prejudice, freedom from the corruption of hate, freedom from the withering blight of pride. Give us that freedom, Father, that seeks the truth, that teaches us our littleness, that brings to us a sense of our ignorance, that realizes how far short we fall of the life we might lead and how far astray we go from the paths that lead to peace, from the paths that lead to righteousness. Make us free with the freedom of the open mind, the freedom of the tender heart, the freedom of the willing hand. Amen.

*The Religion of Mark Twain.*
May 12th, 1918.

# CONFIRMATION CLASS

## CONFIRMATION CLASS

FATHER, in thy will is our peace. Thy will is not far to find nor hard to understand. Thou hast stamped it within our bodies. Thou dost reveal it through our thinking. Thou dost seek us through our loving, and most of all, thou dost ever touch us, now with praise and again with blame, through the divinest revelations of conscience, that mysterious sense of ought that finds us in our sins, that blesses us in our failures.

In thy will we ask for peace. Teach us, thy little children, to realize early that pain and trouble and sorrow and discord, agony of soul and agony of nature are born out of lawlessness, the attempt to evade or defy thy will. Thy will returns in the cycles of the centuries. It is witnessed to in the oblivion that has overwhelmed the defiant, dethroned kings, removed triumphant nations from the fair face of the earth. Thy will has defeated courts and congresses, disgraced parliaments and councils, because they defied and set aside thy law, which is the law of love, of rectitude and of brotherhood. Amen.

*In His Will is our Tranquillity.*
April 30th, 1916.

EACH us, Father, how to pray. Teach us to pursue things noble. Teach us to rise above our weaknesses and cowardice. Make us brave to walk the path of duty. Teach us to trust that voice that speaks of love and peace; of gentleness and service. May we walk the way of helpfulness. Help us to forget ourselves. Help us to rise above the temptations of show and selfishness, help us to realize that we are part and parcel of that cause, represented by those who serve truth and right, and who carry the banners of progress forward. Bless us beyond our power of asking this morning, that we may know the peace that passeth understanding, growing better as we grow older, growing more tender as we grow stronger. Amen.

*The Exemplary Life.*
May 10th, 1914.

# FESTIVAL DAYS

# FESTIVAL DAYS

WITH the rising life of Nature, we would rise to thee, our Father, we would rise to the Infinite Love this morning. As the swelling buds upon the boughs are bursting into beauty, so may our cold-pinched hearts and care-covered lives break into hope. With the singing birds who make glad the spring-time, may our souls carol their larger hopes and diviner joys. Mingled with the beauty of Nature to-day is the diviner beauty of Human Nature. Through the memory of mother-love and father-care we come to realize the motherly arms of the infinite God and the protecting care of the Father in Heaven. We come to this blessed place in heart and spirit to mingle our lives with the heart and spirit of those who, however absent in form, are ever of us and with us. Anew we dedicate this spot to pure purposes and to tender memories. May the sacred dust of the holy ones that guided our feet in the paths of duty, shaped our lives in earnestness and sincerity, make this place more than ever the place of prayer, the house of God, because the home of Love, of Good Will and Fellowship. In the spirit of the teachers and guides of our lives, we would so live that to die is to gain and to live more abundantly in the presence of the Infinite Father and Mother of us all, to whom be kingdom, power and glory forever and ever. Amen.

*Sent to Unity Chapel, Hillside, Wis., with a letter and sermon, Easter, 1889.*

HOSE works that rest upon rectitude; those thoughts that impinge upon truth; those deeds embalmed in love, though dead, Father, thou dost establish. At the threshold of this glad new year, we would realize that none others are established. Out of the past, we would read this one glowing lesson of history, — that thy triumphs rest only upon the virtuous, the sanctities of life come to those who serve. We would realize at this threshold of another opportunity that in so far as aught that is precious and tender in the years gone by is lost, it is lost to selfishness, and so far as it comes to us still redolent with life, pulsing with hope, it comes on the wings of disinterestedness. They who toiled for their own gain are forgotten, lost in the on-rushing stream. They who toiled that others might be more joyous, who testified that others might be free, who lived that others might be happier, they still live in song and story, they still live enshrined in the hearts of the multitude, their names emblazoned upon the imperishable tablets of history. They live most of all in a world made better for their living. So would we gather out of the year that is gone this one precious, sacred lesson for the years to come, — that radiance ever rests upon the brow that loves, that joy ever quickens the feet of those who serve, that strength ever engirdles the soul that is willing to spend and be spent in the service of its kind.

And so in that spirit of Christ-like love, we would welcome this new year and humbly pray

that we may be equal to our opportunities, that
we may be consecrated to our privileges, that life
may receive an onward and upward impetus
through our divine upreachings and outpourings.
Amen.

*New Year's Sermon.*
January 3rd, 1892.

IGHTY Power that bears along the
teeming years, guard within us the
sanctities of memory. We stand this
morning in the presence of the two-
faced angel, knowing not whether to cast our
glance backward in gratitude or forward in devout hopefulness. Father, we welcome the glad
New Year. May our wishes for a happy one be
indeed transmuted into prayer, that divine, ever
answerable prayer that ripens into effort, that is
woven into toil. We come laden with love bless-
ings from the past. May we convert them into
love triumphs in the future and, O Father, as we
stand here this morning weighted down with a
sense of that which we have left undone, timid
in the presence of the mighty tasks that await us,
may thy power come into our lives and lift our
thoughts and our hearts to those heights from
whence ever comes strength, strength to translate
the bequests of the dead into the deeds and the triumphs of the living. In the spirit of the glad season
we would bow before thee and dream of that
happy New Year that can come only to the pure

in heart, the soul that rests upon reality, the heart cradled in love and the mind steadied by a knowledge of the truth. Make us more worthy this glorious century; make us understand the divine significance of living now so that the stars above may beckon us on and ever on to the larger, diviner, more restful life that awaits the trusting spirit. Amen.

*New Year's Sermon.*
January 1st, 1893.

NTO this wealth of goodness we come this morning, Father. May it be with grateful hearts. Into this bounty of love and blessing we have been led. As our hearts go out to thee in great waves of thankfulness for the beautiful things of life, for the generous outpourings of the days and the weeks, may we none the less find gratitude in the thought of the severities that have disappointed, of the hardships that have tempered and the longings that have hallowed and enriched our lives. We thank thee this morning anew for the abundant fields, for the plenty of the harvests, but more for abundant hearts, for the plenty of thought, for the wealth of mind. We thank thee for that guiding conscience that led us through joy and fear, through temptation and weakness, more and more to that perfect light of liberty wherein the soul rejoices continuously in the truth that maketh free, in the love that maketh noble, in the duty that maketh life joyous. Father, we come this morning into the vestibule of this larger home which today we celebrate, grateful for the sweet and holy circle of the inner fireside, none the less grateful that this inner circle finds itself ever related more and more intimately to the larger and still larger circle of city, state and nation, until at last the boundaries of this companionship outreach and take into conscious fellowship the striving and the struggling of all lands and of all places. May thy benedictions fall today upon our hearts to open them wide to these human loves that do so ennoble, and may thy benedictions come in the holy strains of duty as well as in the sweet songs of love. May the cry of the miserable come into our ears today to chasten, to sanctify, and if we will, to beautify the Thanksgiving season, so that by pain, as by pleasure, in sorrow as in joy, we may feel the clasp of heart and hand that holds on now and ever to the eternal verities of life. We bless thee for thy loving providence that permits the gathering of scattered children this week, the reuniting of family circles around the old table and fireside, and none the less, we would remember the providence that has put the vacant chair into the circle; in the memory of that presence felt but not seen, comes the divinest benediction of the family reunion and in the thought of the lost ones comes the greatest wealth of the blessed season. Amen.

*Thanksgiving.*
November 20th, 1892.

AY thy way, O Father, become more clear to us. May we on this day recognize more vividly the indebtedness we owe to thy inspired children; the brave, the great and the true, who in all times and all ages have heralded the light, paved the way for freedom, touched the souls of men with the forces of love, the holy purposes of service. We thank thee, O Father, that we live in a land endowed with holy memories, enriched with the triumphs of martyrs, a land dedicated to thee when it is dedicated to freedom, dedicated to religion when it is dedicated to truth, dedicated to thy holy ones when it is dedicated to progress. Help us, O Father, to do our duty each day and each year that thy kingdom may come more and more efficiently on earth. Amen.

*Washington's Birthday.*
*Thomas Paine, a Friend of*
*Washington.*

February 22nd, 1914.

E thank thee, Father, that out of break- ing hearts blooms the hope of the race. We thank thee that out of the shadows bursts the sunlight. We thank thee that out from under the mountains of snow and ice come ever and anon buttercups and cow- slips. We thank thee that out of the rude and distant past have been born thy chosen ones, upon whose brows fell the light of heaven, who with strength pronounced the words of wisdom that broke the spell of ignorance, lifted cowards into heroes, shamed selfishness into service. We thank thee, Father, for this child of thine, the dear " elder brother " of the American people, the one who, guided by the unerring instincts of justice and love, brought peace out of turmoil and free- dom out of slavery. Father, our thanksgivings fail upon our lips as we break into prayer in our anxiety. We pray for this land of ours, so dis- traught with things unrighteous. We pray for thy people, too much absorbed in things material. Save our country, Father, from sordidness. Save our legislators from the blindness of self seeking. Save our nation from the false lures that reach out after power rather than the divine beckon- ings that reach out after justice. Hasten the day when the message of thy children, thy brave and chosen ones, will be heeded in this land of ours, when we, the inheritors, shall be devoted to the service of mankind, and be inspired with the mighty power of peace, the omnipotence of gentleness, the unquestioned power of kindness.

Wrap us around, O Father, with a sense of law; dedicate us to law; consecrate us to law, that we may be worthy successors of those who toiled, who prayed, who suffered and died that we might be free. Amen.

*Annual Lincoln Sermon.*
*What Would Lincoln Say Were He*
*Living Today.*
February 16th, 1913.

OMPASSED round about by a multitude of witnesses we would lift our souls to thee this morning, Father, in a prayer for liberty, a plea for justice, a cry for brotherhood. Liberty of the mind, justice to things human, brotherhood across the lines of division and antagonism we seek; the brotherhood founded deep in our common parenthood and besetting human-hood, that in justice, in truth and in freedom includes thy children. We would be worthy our great inheritance. Make us members of the immortal band of faithful souls who sought duty in the sunlight of truth. Amen.

*Lincoln Anniversary Sermon.*
*Three Great Supporters, Charles Sumner,*
*Carl Schurz & Lyman Trumbull.*
February 10th, 1918.

ATHER of us all, God of all nations, source of all the sages, thou who hast revealed thyself to us in the mountain peaks of soul, we need some revelation of the high bonds of brotherhood this morning. We need some guidance into the higher realms of fellowship. Father, may the day and the occasion, the theme and the companionship free us from our prejudices and our pride. Save us from the blindness of sect, creed and nationality. Above the din of battle, beyond the hurrahs of the crowd may our ears detect some accent of the eternal gospel that falls from the lips of thy chosen ones, who have lifted the humble, the halting, the blind and the vicious into that serener atmosphere where abides the love that knows no country, ignores all boundaries, yields not primal allegiance to any language, race or sect, but rests in the eternal verities that bind the generations and unite the centuries. Shame us out of a selfish narrow patriotism into the universal brotherhood where we are fellow citizens with the redeemed and the enlightened, the loving, the loyal, the truth telling and the truth serving children of all lands and all climes. We thank thee, Father, for the prophets of all ages. Amen.

*Shakespeare the Revelator.*
*Tercentennial Memorial.*
June 6th, 1916.

NHERITORS of the past we are, Father, recipients of the bounty of those who have gone before. In the consciousness of the rich inheritance that is ours, may we find an abiding love for our fellow-beings, may we find peace in a devotion to the right, in a rising hope for the future. Help us to enter into the life of the miserable, to feel their woes, that thereby we may become better workers with thee for the peace that abideth, the harmony that sweetens bitter hearts, the fellowship that over-reaches the boundaries of rivalry and hate.

Hasten the day, O Father, when man shall no longer lift up hand against his fellowman, when the nations shall recognize their common ties in their common privileges, and work together for the advancement of those things that make for a redeemed world.

Father, we pray that the war-guns may be silenced more speedily, that the hatred in our hearts may be eliminated, that the prejudices born out of ignorance may be dissipated, that the pride of nations and the conceit of flags may be obliterated. We are all thy children and we await thy blessing. Teach us by virtue of our brotherhood to be better citizens of this land, truer advocates of the government which is " of the people, by the people and for the people " forevermore. Amen.

*Battle Field Survivals.*
*A Memorial Day Address.*
May 18th, 1916.

REVEAL to us this morning, Father, the things most worth while; as we look backward into the dark and bloody pages of the past may we discover the stains that have been wiped away and the flowers that have bloomed in their place. May this day, dedicated to holy memories, reveal to us the true heroism, lift us into the higher loyalties. Make us citizens this morning in the republic of peace. Help us to be valiant soldiers in the army that goes forth to save life and conserve the truth. Give us the courage of those who have given their lives that freedom might be more abundantly realized. Give us the courage that enables us to endure hardships, to suffer loneliness, to suffer as with thee in the trials of the camp and hospital. Help us to realize the beauty of our country, the promise of our land, but may this realization bring to us a sense of our responsibility. At a great price has our freedom been bought, may we be worthy of that purchase price by passing this freedom on to new generations, touched with new beauty, sanctified with fresh sacrifices. May the flag of our country gleam more and more with the light that is not on land or sea, the light of love, the light that invites the fraternity of the free, the hunted and the persecuted, aye, the stumbling and erring, wherever they may be. May thy land be our country and thy people our fellow citizens. Amen.

*Annual Memorial Day Sermon.*
*The Post-Bellum Triumphs of The*
*Blue and the Gray.*

May 27th, 1917.

# STUDIES IN MODERN MYSTICISM

ATHER, make us glad that we are here; glad in the communion of souls; glad in the inspirations of thy providence; glad in the revealments of silence; glad in the hope that cannot be cast down; glad in the trust that the Lord reigneth and that his reign is the reign of love; that his law is the law of peace. Father, make us glad of the fellowship of the nations, of the sympathies of religion, the co-operation of thought, the fellowship of mind. Make us glad that we are here to take on new tasks and pledge our fealty to the old. Help us here to keep the light burning that is set on a hill. Help us to be thy children and to worship in thy temple not made with hands. Amen.

*Nature's Triumph Over Death and Decay.*

September 23rd, 1917.

NVISIBLE, ever present, ever working Reality; the substance behind all appearance, the permanent beneath the fleeting and fluctuating, the life behind the song, — we worship thee this morning and in thee find the brotherhood that links the centuries together, unites the ages and extends the bounds of companionship out and beyond all boundaries, down and beneath all differences and entanglements. Thou Infinite One in whose bosom rest the races, the generations, the nationalities, we would worship thee this morning. Amen.

The Bhagavad—*Gita*.
January 6th, 1918.

IN the joy of life, in the power of living, we give thanks this morning. May we recognize, Father, the mighty sweep of thy providence, the on-flowing life of thy universe, that with storm and sunshine, winter snows and summer flowers, links together the seasons, holds in a common bond the planets, ties in one embrace all the children of men. Help us to realize that this is an " age on ages telling that to be living is sublime." Forgotten be the things that divide as we live in the presence of the infinite life, which reveals itself in ever changing forms and ever growing ideals, found in the thoughts and loves of men. Amen.

*The Brahmo Somaj.*
*The New Hinduism of the East.*
January 13th, 1918.

NTO this upper chamber, Father, may there come this morning a sweet sense of brotherhood with all things fair and good. May there come into our hearts a sense of brooding power, breaking into the crystal glory of the snowflake, making it kin to the sweeping planets. In this upper chamber this morning may there come into our hearts a sense of divine presence seeking expression in our highest thought, seeking embodiment in our noblest words as we bow before the inexpressible and ineffable altars of the most lowly as well as the Most High. Amen.

*Theosophy.*
*A New Hinduism of the West.*
January 20th, 1918.

O thy will, Father, we would set our wills this morning; thy will as it breaks upon us in the beauty and glory of this wintry day; thy will as it comes to us in the prayers and sacrifices of thy noblest children; thy will as it comes to us in the fierce agony of thy suffering ones, protesting against our cruelty, pleading with our humanity. To thy will, Father, we would set our wills this morning that we may become conscious members of the unbroken harmony of man, that we may be partakers of that inspiration that follows the sunshine around the world and that we may be inheritors of thy revelations that have broken upon the minds of men in many climes and in many tongues. We ask for

a new sense of brotherhood, a fresh revelation of
the things that unite. Help us, Father, to set our
faces against the things that divide. We would
banish hate from our hearts, eliminate the
thoughts that blight our souls. In sackcloth and
ashes we bow before thee today and confess our
cruelty, recognize the wrongs we inflict. Make
us better brothers and sisters for our having been
here. Amen.

> *The Bahai Movement.*
> *A Free Religious Movement in*
> *the East.*
> January 27th, 1918.

NFINITE TENDERNESS, Eternal
Power, Unfailing Law and Ever Present Love! Thus with human phrases
and inclusive words we seek thee, the
Ineffable, and would fain realize thine infinite
presence. We would know thy will, we would
revere thy realities, we would stand in thy holy
temple of matter, touched anew with the awe
that comes to the soul that realizes immensity.
Through it may we be touched anew with rever-
ence for the soul that catches glimpses of the inevitable sweep of thy will, revealed in the swing-
ing planets and the returning seasons, revealed in
the delicate architecture of body and the supreme
mysteries of the soul. Thus seeking we would
worship thee, Father, this morning. Amen.

> *Christian Science.*
> *Neo-Buddhism in the West.*
> February 3rd, 1918.

ENEATH the turmoil and the con-
flict, beneath the worry and the hate,
beyond the passing phase of things we
would find thee, the eternal Calm, the
undisturbed Power, the besetting Love. Behind
the noblest words we would find still higher,
nobler thought, above the highest deeds we would
find still higher purposes. Touch us with a sense
of our humanity this morning, Father, help us to
recognize our finiteness, the inadequacy of words,
the feebleness of phrases. Help us to commune
with thee in the spirit of the noble, the faithful,
the serving and the suffering children of thine.
Amen.

*The "New Thought" and Other Cults.*
February 17th, 1918.

N the silence of this holy opportunity,
in the quiet of this place of escape
from the hurry and the noise, the fever
and the hates of life, in the sweetness
of the perception of truth, love and duty, we
would worship this morning. Father, we dare
take upon our lips words, poor broken counters
of thought; phrases, inadequate measurement of
feeling, in the hope that they help us to catch
some fresh glimpse of thy presence, feel the new
throb of thy life, awaken a new sense of thy
nearness, bring a revelation to our finite eyes.
Amen.

*Realizing God. The Awakened Life.*
February 24th, 1918.

# ANTI-WAR

# ANTI-WAR

*Love For the Battle-Torn Nations*

ATHER, help us, standing this morning in the foremost files of time, to feel the beauty and the glory of our inheritance, the strength and power that thy providence poured into our veins at birth. Help us to realize with grateful hearts that we opened our eyes on this world-wonder with our eyes already focused for beauty. Help us to realize that when first this universe broke upon our ears they were tuned to melody, already committed to harmony, and that when these minds of ours first undertook the high and mystic tasks of thinking, our brains were already organized for wisdom, trained to reason. We thank thee for this inheritance through eye, ear and heart. Heirs of all the past, may we be children not of today or of this place, but children of the ages and citizens of the world. Amen.

*Why Love England?*
October 3rd, 1915.

OR the saints and the seers of the ages, we give thanks. For the freedom that was bought for us at a great price by those who have gone before, we give thanks. For the illuminated wisdom of the pioneers and the leaders of men, we give thanks this morning.

Broaden our vision, Father. Help us to see beyond the murky clouds of suffering and hatred. Help us to look up, Father, and see the radiant faces of those who in times of trouble sang the songs of love, who in the dissonance of war declared the gospel of peace. For thy great children whose words have come down through the ages, the radiance of whose faces illuminated the dark places of history, O God, for these we give thanks and we pray that we may find release from the narrow bonds of land and language. Help us this morning to become citizens of the world. Amen.

*Why Love Germany?*
October 10th, 1915.

AKE us citizens of the world this morning, Father, by touching our hearts with love for all thy struggling children, by quickening our minds with appreciation of all the tribes of earth that have stumbled towards the light, groping towards love, and out of their failure have made stepping stones upon which those who come after them may climb a little nearer to the goal, the home and hope of man. Make us simple, sincere, earnest. Help us to see through the sham and glitter of the hour, and plant our feet on the everlasting rock of duty, justice, freedom and progress which thou dost ever vouchsafe to thy seeking children. Amen.

*Why Love France?*
October 17th, 1915.

NLARGE our hearts this morning, Father. Show us the wider range of thy love as revealed through the ages, witnessed to by the loyalty shown in the lives and deaths of thy chosen ones in all lands and under all names. Soften our hearts, put therefrom all hatred. When our souls stagger under the weight of wrong and cruelty, of bloodshed and hate, save us, Father, from swelling the curse by adding hatred to hate.

Help us to see that our hatred is born from our own ignorance rather than from the vice of others.

We pray for all thy wayward and wandering children. Forgive them, Father, for they know not what they do. Amen.

*Why Love Italy?*
October 25th, 1915.

ENLARGE our minds this morning, Father, open our hearts to more wisdom, lead our feet in the way of understanding that we may behold thy glory, made manifest in the works of man; that we may discover thy law showing itself in the triumphs of nations; that we may feel thy presence in the struggling children of men. Make us more just, the one to the other; enable us to see things not only from the standpoint of our narrow and selfish interests, but, in so far as is possible, through the exercise of reason and the practice of love. May we see things as they appear to those whom we distrust, those whom we abase, those to whom we deny the right of private judgment and individual vision. Father, make us more kindly the one to the other. Help us to see beneath the coarse, the harsh, the cruel, and discover ever the growing power of love, moving towards tenderness, ripening into helpfulness. We bless thee for the radiance of the sunshine and the greater radiance of the love that streams through the centuries. Amen.

*Why Love Russia?*
November 7th, 1915.

AKE us glad that we are alive this morning, Father, glad for the sunshine and the clouds, glad for pleasure and for pain. We thank thee that thou hast given us the power to suffer and to rise above the things that thwart our growth. We thank thee for the peace which is ever found in thee. Lift us into the comradeship of the brave, into the fellowship of the struggling. Open our hearts to new loves. Open our minds to new truths. Quicken our hearts to new errands of mercy. Touch our hearts with fresh tenderness that we may know the peace that passeth understanding, thy peace that abideth now and forevermore. Amen.

*Why Love Turkey?*
November 14th, 1915.

NTO that overarching consciousness that has touched with awe the groping souls of men in all times and in all places, we would enter this morning, Father. We would enter in such a spirit that we may realize that our lives are related the one to the other; and that in this bond which binds each to each there is found that diviner link that connects all men and all nations to thee, — the immeasurable Love, the unfathomable Care, the inscrutable Power that holdeth the planets in their places and telleth the stars by their names and comforteth the broken in heart.

Infinite Presence, in this comforting sense of thy nearness, we would read the ways of thy providence to the men of far off times and far off lands, the tender consciousness of being one with nature, one with prophetic, noble souls of all lands who have lifted temptation and sin from off burdened souls. Lift us into this glad communion, by the old and ever new way of worship, by the blessed road of thought, by the divine highway of love, making this home-land of ours a vestibule to that great temple wherein the unbroken family of man will worship now and evermore. Amen.

*Above All Nations is Humanity.*
November 21st, 1915.

ATHER, out of abundant hearts we pour our gratitude to that providence that in its mysterious weavings has brought us here again; once more we meet in the full tides of love and companionship and the solemn call of duty. Once more we are confronted by the unspeakable, the immeasurable opportunities of service. Service to thy suffering children of men, service to the abiding causes, so thwarted by the confusion of the hour; service to thee, the God of love.

Help us to stand consciously in the presence of things eternal, realizing the infinite sweep of thy law, mindful of the slow evolution of the centuries. Help us to rise above the distractions of the hour; make us deaf to the clamor of the day; release us from the tyranny of the years and the age, that we may stand with the prophets that know not time but eternity. Thus we may be in league with the ages that through turmoil and travail spell the message of peace.

Help us to realize that we are ministers of justice, members of the struggling family of man. Forgotten be land and flag and country today in the nobler memories of the all-fatherland of humanity, the agonizing thirst for peace that is the burden of our brothers and sisters beyond the pale of country, beyond the lure of the flag. Above all may we see floating the white banners of peace and above the dissonance of war hear the angelic anthems of "Peace on earth, goodwill to men." Amen.

*The Peace Pilgrimage Across the Sea.*
*Did It Pay?*

March 5th, 1916.

BE still, O my soul, that I may hear the voice of my God, speaking to me in the deep silences that lie behind speech and beyond all action. Be silent, O ye clamorous wants, this morning, that I may feel the tug of soul toward thee, the Infinite. Forgotten be the petty words of pride in home and country this morning, in the greater words of humanity.

Father, help us to bend the knee before the altar of the Infinite Life that reveals itself in many tongues and has not left man without a witness of thee at any time or in any clime. May thy peace come to us, may thy peace brood over thy wayward children. Touch them with humility, quicken them with remorse over their relentless defiance to the still small voice that breaks through the roar of a cannon, that rides upon the storm, speaking ever the words, " Peace, be still, and know that I am God." Amen.

*The United States On Trial.*
February 4th, 1917.

UT of our agony we cry to thee this morning, thou the Infinite Love, thou the undying Potency that makes for righteousness. Thou to whom we hasten to find a listening ear, who listens to the wail of the widow, the cry of the orphan, who hearest the groans of the mangled. O thou Infinite Tenderness, we cry to thee in the heart of thy children, we plead with thee in the decision of councils and cabinets. We would approach thee through congresses and parliaments. Save thy children from the infidelity that distrusts thee, save the nations from the atheism that denies thy potency, O thou Infinite Love. Lift us out of our cowardly doubts, give us a place in the inner heaven of faith, give us courage to speak the words of tenderness, to trust beyond the sight and where the vision cannot go, — " that no good thing is failure and no evil thing success." No cause of truth can be advanced by evil, no claim of right can be settled by wrong, cumulating wrong. Give us the peace that comes to trusting souls, the peace of those who dare refuse the path of violence, who turn away from the resort to violence and distrust, the power of might in their great and abounding faith in right. Amen.

*The Gift of Tongues—Pentecost.*
February 18th, 1917.

ELP us this morning, Father, to feel the burdens of the world. Bless us if need be, with agony that thereby we may come into kinship with things eternal, that we may be allied to the causes that are everlasting. Teach us through pain and sorrow and death if need be, the unbreakable ties of brotherhood. Help us to feel the golden links in that chain that binds us to the meanest, links us with the lowliest, makes us conscious brothers with the wickedest. For in our own lives do we find the weakness and the wickedness, the selfishness and the greed, the coarseness, the vulgarity that the ages have striven to escape from. We pray for our distracted country. Hasten the day when its banners shall again wave over peaceful citizens. Bring into our homes the power to endure hardness if need be in the interest of the right. Our hearts go out to the faithful and the

loyal who in any garb or for any cause have consecrated their young lives to thee. Preserve them
in their purity, hold them to their ideals, teach
them love, more love which alone overcometh
pain, and triumphs in the interest of good. Amen.

*The Reassurances of the Past.*
September 30th, 1917.

# FUNERALS

# FUNERAL PRAYERS

*At the Funeral of a Grandmother*

NFINITE TENDERNESS, we thank thee that thou hast given thy weary child rest. We thank thee for the long procession of years, the overflowing months in which thy child communed with thee and during which her spirit drank of thy bounty. We thank thee for the mind that could look before and after, the open-eyed mind that could take note of thy Providence weaving the fabric of history in her presence. We thank thee for those moments of vision when the eye was clear to see things supernal and to enjoy glimpses of the celestial realm wherein broods the eternal love. We thank thee for the ties of fellowship that wove this loyal daughter into the companionship of home and church. We thank thee, Father, that thou didst minister to her through the word of the prophet and the message of the poet, that thou didst strengthen her through the consolations of the altar and the duties of the fireside. We thank thee that after long service thou hast given her the benediction of a serene old age, that now, the day's work well done, the burdens well borne, the weakness and the loneliness heroically endured, she has sunk to rest surrounded by loving and loyal ones. May she who wrought so well rest well in the eternal arms. May her memory abide with us; may her example remain in our midst; may her affection still enrich our hearts, sweeten our lives.

Father, comfort and strengthen the mourning ones so that they too may, in thine own way, and in thine own time, pass out of the seen into the eternal presence and feel the clasp of the everlasting arms. Amen.

September 29th, 1914.

## At the Funeral of the Elevator Man at Lincoln Centre

E thank thee, Father, that thou hast taken home thy child; that after life's fitful waking thou hast given thy beloved sleep. We thank thee for the leadings of thy children into ways of pleasantness and paths of peace. We thank thee, that thou hast put thy homeless ones into homes; hast given to thy solitary ones companionship.

We thank thee for the life of simple loyalty lived by this child of patience. May our hearts be made more tender, more loyal, more willing to serve for the tutoring by this fellow mortal, this co-worker, this child of thine and brother of ours.

We remember ties that reach out and beyond our knowledge and our acquaintance. Wherever they may be, may those who claim kinship with this our brother be sweetened and strengthened by the assurance of a life well lived and a grave well earned. Amen.

January 21st, 1912.

*At the Funeral of a Mother*

OMFORT thy children, Father, in this hour of thoughtfulness and gratefulness, sanctified by sorrow. Comfort thy children with the tender memories of the past, the holy associations of long and loving years. Wrap them round about with the mantle of thy love, enable them to see through the mists and vapors of these earthly damps. When the eyes are washed clear by tears may they catch glimpses of heaven's eternal lamps.

Comfort thy children, O God, with a sense of thy nearness, thy infinity, thy all-Fatherhood. Pluck from our hearts the wavering distrust, plant instead the faith that blooms into hope and beauty which enables us on the shores of time to catch glimpses of the lights of eternity.

We thank thee for the gentle life, the kindly spirit, the guiding hand that in ways she knew not of, sanctified this world, glorified this home, purified hearts and strengthened tempted wills. Amen.

April 15th, 1918.

*At the Funeral of a*
*Civil War Comrade*

NFINITE TENDERNESS, Giver of Love, Source of Truth and Justice, we thank thee that thou hast taken home thy child; that after the years of faithful service thou hast given rest. We thank thee for this revelation of thyself. In him has fatherhood been interpreted; in him the love of the home has anticipated the love of Heaven.

We thank thee that thou hast brought us into thy presence by this visitation of thine angel whom we call death. Help us to feel that this life is part and parcel of the unending world that moves ever towards life, more beauty, fuller love.

May the holy remembrances of the past chasten the souls of those present. Strengthen the purposes and renew the hopes of the future, O God. Thy peace, Father, thou hast given to thy child. May we know of thy peace this morning, the peace that passeth understanding, the peace that abideth now and forevermore. Amen.

August 9th, 1917.

## At the Funeral of a Little Boy

INFINITE TENDERNESS, touch us with a sense of the beauty of life. Help us to see through our tears the meaning of life. Tutor us through our sorrows, Father, into the companionship that endures. May thy peace that passeth understanding, the peace that is his, be ours in thine own good time and thine own good way.

Help us to dedicate this spot, sacred in our memories as the resting place of all that is mortal of him who is not here but has arisen. May the glory of thy law and the beauty of thy truth be interpreted in terms of love and patience, of faith and endurance, now and evermore. Amen.

September 21st, 1912.

## At the Funeral of a Violinist

INFINITE NEARNESS, Eternal Tenderness, whose ways are beyond finding out but whose decrees are ever just, whose laws are ever divine. O thou Father of us all, teach us the lessons of life, sweeten to us the trials of earth, chasten our sorrows into power, convert our griefs into courage. Help us to lay hold of the timeless things and to feel that we are in the realm of the permanent, that the unseen are the things eternal. The seen is transient, the things of sense are changeable, but the things of truth and love abide now and forevermore. May our hearts be touched with beauty, the beauty of the things hoped for and struggled for, the beauty of the dawn, the beauty of things not realized. Touch us with a sense of the cords that bind us each to each and all to thee. So lift us to the heights of gratitude that we may sing in our hearts songs of praise for the revelation of thyself that came to us through this child of thine. We thank thee that thou didst give to us some echoes of the eternal music through her hands. We thank thee that thou didst unstop our ears that we might hear some of thy harmonies through her, thine interpreter. Amen.

Tower Hill.
6:30 A.M.
July 30th, 1912.

# MISCELLANEOUS

## MISCELLANEOUS PRAYERS

TUTOR us this morning, O Father, with the words of thy chosen ones, who in times past have followed the light. Tutor us with the kindly helps of near and dear ones. Help us to feel the bonds that bind each to each and all to thee. Help us to hear the cry of the lonely, the wail of the suffering. Help us to enter into the sorrows of broken homes, that through sorrow and tears we may find the way to thee, the life of love and the love of life. Tutor us through the yearnings of our own hearts, through the gleam that penetrates the darkness in our own minds, and above all through that still small voice which is never entirely silent, which whispers from within of duty and love, of purposes unrealized, of hopes unspeakable, of triumphs that await thy children whenever they are consecrated by the lessons of the past to the needs of the present, and to the guidings of the inner life, which is thy life within the souls of thy children. Amen.

*Why Go To Church On Sunday?*
*The Bible Lesson.*

April 19th, 1914.

THOU Refuge of souls! Thou who art a shelter in a waste land! Who art nourishment to hungry souls! We, thy children, groping toward light, staggering in our way toward the right, we bless thee, this morning, for the guidance of the past. We would thank thee not only for the bounty of the field, the corn and the fruit that perisheth, but we would thank thee for that nourishment of the heart, that food of the mind, that Providence of the spirit which has sustained us at our tasks, which has reinforced us in our discouragements, which has steadied us when we wavered.

Unseen though ever present, unknown though forever realized, unspeakable Father, in thee we live, in thee we move, in thee we have our being. Help us to withdraw from the clamor of the outside, the clatter of tongues that speak things outward, that belong to the passing show of things, that we may rest in thee, the Eternal, abide in thee, the Unchangeable and the Everlasting. May we attune our spirits this morning to Heavenly music that we may shape our lives more faithfully to celestial things. Help us to realize that we are in thy presence, that the present moment is part of thine infinite realities. Chasten us by silence, purify us by meditation, console us by the baptism of thine own spirit that bringest rest in life, peace in turmoil, faith out of doubt. Amen.

*The True Lent.*
February 25th, 1917.

E thank thee that ever and anon thou hast allowed thy children to climb the mount of vision, to see the wider horizon, and to hear the higher call that will enable them to realize the things that are not necessary, to select between the transient and the permanent, to choose the lasting, not the fleeting things of life.

We stand on this mortal ledge of time hearing the break of the waves of eternity on either hand, the measureless past calling to the measureless future. The short measure of life of our days enables us to see some things that are worth while, to discover some things that are very dear to thee and consequently dear to thy children. Touch us with only so much loyalty of memory as will equip us for the future. We pray that we may see our opportunity to do good as in days gone. Forbid that we should rest in idle confidence on things accomplished. Forbid that we would, having placed our hands to the plough, look back. Rebuke us, Father, whenever we are disposed to boast what we have done and to offer it as an excuse for indifference in the future.

Father, we bless thee for the fellowship of this gathering; we thank thee that thou hast permitted us to work together, but we pray that the working hour may be continued, that when night comes we may retire without discouraging those who come after us. Bless these little ones who are to take our places. Save the generations that are to come by consecration, holy purposes, and high ideals. Banish the plenty that cripples and weakens. Hasten the blight of that wealth that destroys. Consecrate us anew to new enterprises and new undertakings now and forevermore, that we may be still on the marching line, still on duty, still looking to the future, still striving to achieve. Amen.

*Thirtieth Anniversary of All Souls Church.*
November 3rd, 1912.